George Washington Carver:

Agriculture Pioneer

by Stephanie Macceca

Science Contributor
Sally Ride Science
Science Consultants
Thomas R. Ciccone, Science Educator
Ronald Edwards, Science Educator

MISSION: SCIENCE

Sally Ride
Science

3 1907 00246 2769

First hardcover edition published in 2010 by
Compass Point Books
151 Good Counsel Drive
P.O. Box 669
Mankato, MN 56002-0669

Editor: Anthony Wacholtz
Designer: Heidi Thompson
Editorial Contributor: Robin Doak
Media Researcher: Svetlana Zhurkin
Production Specialist: Jane Klenk

 This book was manufactured with paper containing at least 10 percent post-consumer waste.

Library of Congress Cataloging-in-Publication Data
Macceca, Stephanie.
  George Washington Carver : agriculture pioneer / by Stephanie Macceca.
      p. cm.—(Mission: science)
  Includes index.
  ISBN 978-0-7565-4305-1 (library binding)
  1. Carver, George Washington, 1864?–1943—Juvenile literature.
  2. African American agriculturists—Biography—Juvenile literature.
  3. Agriculturists—United States—Biography—Juvenile literature.
  I. Title. II. Series.
  S417.C3M23 2010
  630.92—dc22   2009034855

Visit Compass Point Books on the Internet at *www.compasspointbooks.com*
or e-mail your request to *custserv@compasspointbooks.com*

Table of Contents

Humble Beginnings

Born into slavery, George Washington Carver struggled against prejudice and poverty to become one of the most important agricultural scientists of his time. Carver is most famous for his research on peanuts and other types of plants. He taught students and farmers the benefits of good agricultural practices, including crop rotation. He spent a lifetime looking for ways to improve the lives of poor farmers in the South and other parts of the United States.

One of Carver's greatest achievements was advancing the cause of African-American people. At a time when racism was common in the United States, Carver showed that blacks could achieve success. He spent much of his life educating young black students at the Tuskegee Normal and Industrial Institute in Alabama.

Peanut Power

Carver encouraged Southern farmers to plant peanuts because they added important nutrients to the soil. He also knew that peanuts were a good source of protein for humans and livestock.

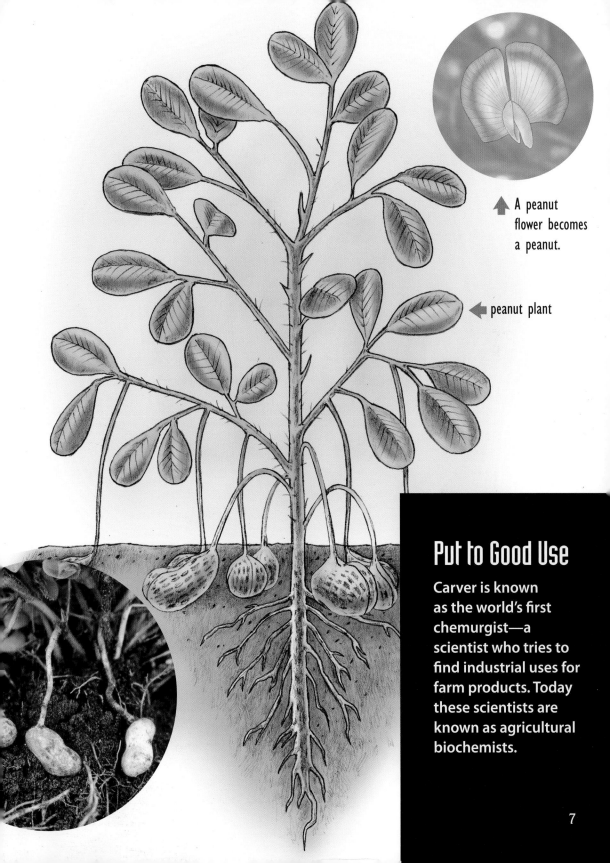

A peanut flower becomes a peanut.

peanut plant

Put to Good Use

Carver is known as the world's first chemurgist—a scientist who tries to find industrial uses for farm products. Today these scientists are known as agricultural biochemists.

Born a Slave

George Washington Carver was born into slavery on a small farm near Diamond Grove, Missouri, just before the end of the Civil War (1861–1865). George's mother, Mary, was a slave owned by a couple named Moses and Susan Carver. Although the couple did not approve of slavery, they still owned slaves to work on their farm. George's father may have been a slave on a nearby farm.

When George was just an infant, slave raiders kidnapped him and his mother. The kidnappers planned to make money by selling them in another state. Moses Carver hired a neighbor to search for the two.

The neighbor found George abandoned along a roadside in Arkansas. Mary was never found. Moses and his wife

Slaves were used to harvest cotton and other crops.

decided to raise George and his brother, Jim. Because George was a weak and sickly child, he couldn't work in the fields. So Susan Carver taught him to cook, sew, and help with the laundry. She also taught him how to read. The young boy was a quick learner who was curious about the world around him. He collected rocks and plants from nearby forests to study and sketch.

What Is an Abolitionist?

For many years, slavery was legal in the United States. Abolitionists were people who believed that slavery was wrong and should be outlawed. They worked to abolish slavery, which means to do away with it.

▲ Frederick Douglass was a well-known abolitionist.

Birthday Mystery

Because the birth dates of slaves often were not recorded properly, it is impossible to know exactly when Carver was born. He sometimes offered two dates—January 1864 and January 1865.

Early Education

Because he was black, George was not allowed to attend the public school in Diamond Grove. At that time, schools in Missouri and many other states were segregated by race. When he was about 11 years old, George moved to the nearby town of Neosho to go to school in a small, one-room schoolhouse. In Neosho, he lived with a black couple named Andrew and Mariah Watkins. He earned his keep by helping with household chores.

▼ African-American students at a blacks-only school

Mariah Watkins made an important impression on young George. She encouraged him to learn as much as possible, and then to find a way to give his knowledge back to other people. George took these words to heart.

George continued to be fascinated by nature. He collected specimens of plants and insects. He learned how water and nutrients from the soil are carried from a plant's roots to its leaves. He experimented to find out what types of soil and nutrients were best for certain kinds of plants.

Few Resources

George learned to read using the only books available in the Carver home: *Webster's Elementary Spelling Book* and the Bible. By the time he left the Carvers' home at the age of 11 or 12, he had nearly memorized the spelling book.

Where the W came from

When George lived in Ames, Iowa, it was home to another man named George Carver. To set himself apart from this man, he began signing his letters "George W. Carver." When asked what the "W" stood for, Carver told people "Washington."

Did You Know?

Young George often helped his neighbors nurse their sick plants back to health. His friends called him the Plant Doctor, a nickname that stuck with him for the rest of his life.

Elizabeth Britton
(1858—1934)

At a time when few women pursued careers in science, Elizabeth Britton was an exception. Born in New York City, Britton was brought up on a sugar plantation in Cuba. Like Carver, she was interested in plants and science from an early age.

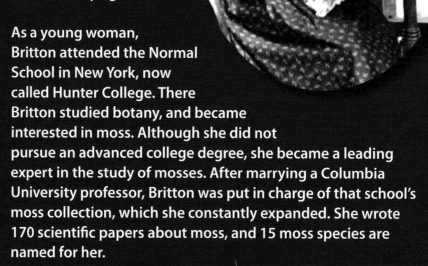

As a young woman, Britton attended the Normal School in New York, now called Hunter College. There Britton studied botany, and became interested in moss. Although she did not pursue an advanced college degree, she became a leading expert in the study of mosses. After marrying a Columbia University professor, Britton was put in charge of that school's moss collection, which she constantly expanded. She wrote 170 scientific papers about moss, and 15 moss species are named for her.

Britton also worked to preserve wildflowers. In 1891 she helped found the New York Botanical Garden, and her husband became the garden's first director. In 1893 Britton was the only woman nominated to be a founding member of the Botanical Society of America. Britton died in the Bronx, New York, when she was 76 years old.

Kansas

When George was about 13, he moved with some neighbors to Fort Scott, Kansas. He hoped to receive a better education there. George did whatever he could to earn money for himself. When he had money, he went to school. When he ran out of money, he worked.

Then George lived with the Seymours in Olathe, Kansas. Lucy Seymour taught him how to iron ruffles and pleats on fancy clothes. He moved with the family to Minneapolis, Kansas, where he attended high school.

After graduating, George applied to Highland College in Kansas, and he was accepted. When he arrived to sign up for courses, however, he was rudely turned away. The college did not accept black students. This was a serious setback for the young man.

Fashion of the time was complex and detailed. Ironing such garments, as Carver did, would have been complicated work.

Art or Science

Although discouraged, Carver applied to Simpson College in Indianola, Iowa, to study art. He was accepted, and he became the college's first African-American student. Life as a student was difficult. After paying his college costs, Carver had little money to live on. For a month, he ate only beef suet and cornmeal.

Although Carver had talent as an artist, one of his teachers encouraged him to try a different path. The teacher saw that the young man had a natural way with plants. She suggested that he study botany instead of art. Carver took her advice. In 1891 he transferred to Iowa State College in Ames to study agricultural science. Today the college is called Iowa State University.

 Carver was in the National Guard Student Battalion at what is now Iowa State University.

Did You Know?

Carver entered a drawing contest at the Chicago World's Fair in 1893. He won an honorable mention for a painting called *Yucca and Cactus*.

Katherine Esau
(1898—1997)

Katherine Esau was one of the greatest plant biologists of the 20th century. Esau studied the anatomy of plants. Her books *Plant Anatomy* and *Anatomy of Seed Plants* are still considered two of the most important books about plants ever written.

Esau was born in Ukraine. When she was 18, she entered a women's agricultural college in Moscow, Russia. There she studied natural sciences, chemistry, physics, and geology. Although her studies were interrupted by the Russian Revolution and World War I, she eventually earned a degree in plant breeding in Germany.

When Esau was 24, she and her family moved to Reedley, California. Over the next nine years, Esau worked and continued her studies. She spent much of her time developing a sugar beet plant that could resist diseases. In 1931 she was awarded a doctorate by the University of California at Berkeley.

Esau devoted the rest of her life to studying and teaching about plants, especially crop plants. In 1957 she became the sixth woman ever elected to the National Academy of Sciences. And at age 91, she received the National Medal of Science, an important and prestigious award. Esau died in California at the age of 99.

Life at Iowa State College was not easy for Carver. Although college officials had accepted him as their first black student, there were many things he was not allowed to do. He could not live in the dormitories or eat meals with white students. Instead he had to sleep in an old office and eat his meals with college employees in the dining hall basement.

Despite the discrimination and prejudice he faced, Carver studied hard and excelled at the college. He learned how pollen works in plants. He also learned about crossbreeding plants to create new and better species of plants and flowers.

◄ Farmers must understand soil and its nutrients in order to grow healthy crops.

Carver learned how to apply science to farming in other ways, too. He studied the makeup of soil and how nutrients in the soil affect plant growth. One subject that fascinated him was plant diseases and how they might be prevented.

David Grandison Fairchild [1869—1954]

Plant explorer David Grandison Fairchild spent his life traveling the world, looking for new plant species and varieties to bring to the United States. As an employee of the U.S. Department of Agriculture, Fairchild helped introduce more than 80,000 species and varieties of plants to the United States. He brought the first flowering cherry trees from Japan in 1906. He also introduced mangoes, pistachios, nectarines, bamboo, and horseradish.

After Fairchild retired in 1933, he and his family moved to Coconut Grove, Florida. He worked to establish a national park in the Everglades. In 1938 he published a book about his adventures as a plant explorer, titled *The World Was My Garden*.

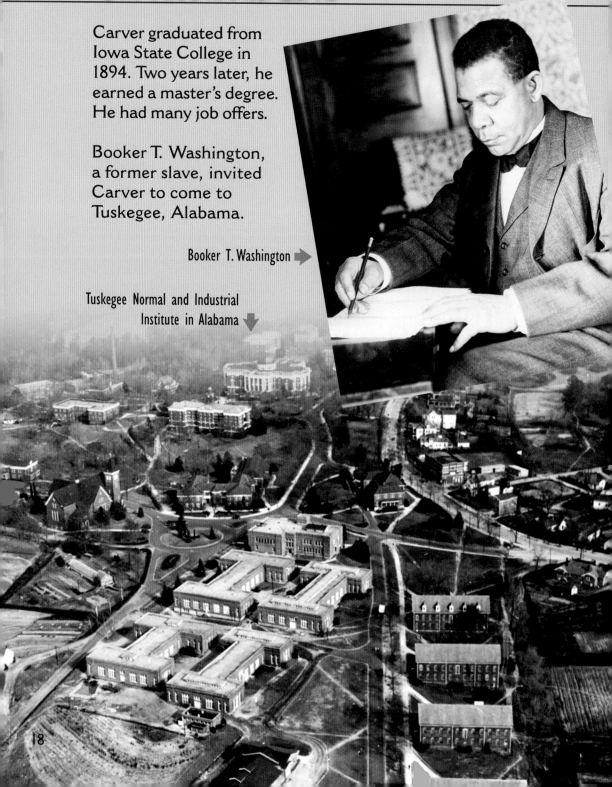

Carver graduated from Iowa State College in 1894. Two years later, he earned a master's degree. He had many job offers.

Booker T. Washington, a former slave, invited Carver to come to Tuskegee, Alabama.

Booker T. Washington ➤

Tuskegee Normal and Industrial Institute in Alabama ⬇

In 1881 Washington had been the driving force in creating the Tuskegee Normal and Industrial Institute. The school taught academic and practical subjects to African-American students.

Washington asked Carver to be the director of the school's agriculture department. He believed it was important for black people to support themselves and to own land. Washington thought Carver could help accomplish this mission by teaching students and farmers better planting and growing techniques.

When Carver arrived in Tuskegee, he saw that the land there was eroded and barren. The cotton crops were small and sickly. He immediately knew that the farmers there needed to grow other types of crops.

Tuskegee Courses

Students at Tuskegee were taught skills they could use to make a living. Courses were offered in carpentry, tailoring, shoemaking, printing, and cabinetmaking. Some of the first buildings at the school were built with bricks made by students in brick-making courses.

No Resources Again

Carver's first task at Tuskegee was to create a usable laboratory. Because the agriculture building was not finished, he had to teach in a shack with no heat. He had no supplies except for his own microscope, a gift from his friends at Iowa State. So Carver and his students collected items such as pots, pans, tubes, fruit jars, and wires to make their own equipment. Carver believed it was important to save everything and to waste nothing.

Carver's next task was to clean up the land around the

school. The institute was located on an abandoned plantation, but the land was swampy, with a lot of trash. The soil was mostly dry clay, and few flowers or shrubs grew there. Carver and his students cleared the trash from the land and prepared it for planting healthy crops.

The History of Peanut Butter

Peanut butter has been around for much longer than you'd think. The ancient Incans of South America were known to have made a paste of peanuts. Carver promoted peanut recipes, including three for peanut butter, so he is sometimes incorrectly credited with its invention. The first person to patent a method of making peanut butter in the United States was Dr. John Harvey Kellogg in 1895.

◄ Carver and his students conducted agricultural research.

New Method of Teaching

When Carver came to Tuskegee, most students learned by attending lectures, reading books, and memorizing vocabulary. Carver thought that students who studied science this way didn't really understand plants. He believed he had a better way to teach students about botany and agriculture.

Carver believed in hands-on learning. His students performed experiments and evaluated the results. Carver took his students on nature walks and showed them things they needed to know about.

Carver also wanted to teach Alabama farmers how to improve their land. He knew that these farmers were too busy to come to school. So using a large horse-drawn wagon, Carver took learning to the farmers. Once a month, he drove his school on wheels, the Jesup agricultural wagon, to local farms. He and his students demonstrated the latest techniques in planting and growing.

▲ Carver's "movable school"

Emma Lucy Braun
(1889–1971)

Even as a young child, Emma Lucy Braun loved plants. Braun's parents, both teachers, often took her and her older sister Annette into the forests of Ohio to look and learn. Her mother kept a collection of pressed wildflowers that the two sisters often studied.

After graduating from college with a doctorate in botany, Braun teamed up with her sister. Annette was now an entomologist, a scientist who studies insects. The two moved to a house in the Ohio woods. They studied the forest around them and became experts on woodland ecology. They even had their own laboratory, called the "science wing."

As a professor of botany and a dedicated researcher, Braun earned the respect of those who loved nature. She wrote several books about her observations and findings, and four plants were named after her. In 1950 she became the first female president of the Ecological Society of America.

Carver wrote, edited, and printed 44 pamphlets that offered farming advice to poor farmers, along with practical uses for crops such as peanuts and sweet potatoes. Many of his recipes can be found on the Internet.

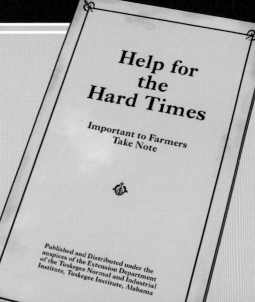

Help for the Hard Times

Important to Farmers
Take Note

Published and Distributed under the auspices of the Extension Department of the Tuskegee Normal and Industrial Institute, Tuskegee Institute, Alabama

Corn Plastics

Another plant that has many uses is corn. Did you know that corn can be used to make plastic? Unlike plastics made with petroleum, corn plastic is renewable and breaks down over time.

Items that can be made from corn plastic include trash bags, shopping bags, plastic cups, and disposable eating utensils. Golf tees, pillow stuffing, and greeting cards are also made with this eco-friendly substance. You might even be listening to your favorite music on a player made partly from corn plastic! In the 1980s, some electronics industry leaders began using such plastic for the casings of their products.

Carver found more than 300 uses for the peanut. People nicknamed him The Peanut Man. Some of the things he created or proposed making from the peanut include:

- chili sauce
- bleach
- metal polish
- cosmetics
- paper
- glue
- linoleum
- axle grease
- pavement
- cloth dye
- instant coffee
- mayonnaise
- shaving cream
- paint
- fuel briquettes
- gasoline
- medicines
- plastics
- ink
- wood stains
- rubber
- shoe polish

Carver could have made a lot of money from his discoveries. But he believed that God inspired and guided his work. He thought his discoveries belonged to everyone. Carver only applied for three patents to protect his discoveries from unfair use by other people. One of the patents was for a face cream made from ground peanuts.

Carver used many techniques to turn peanut plants into useful products.

The Wizard of Tuskegee

Inventor Thomas Alva Edison wanted Carver to work for him. Edison offered Carver a large salary and his own well-stocked laboratory. But the Wizard of Tuskegee, as he was called by then, turned down the job offer.

The carmaker Henry Ford also admired Carver. Both men were very interested in making fuels from grains. Today these are known as biofuels. Ford and Carver wrote letters back and forth, discussing industrial uses for soybeans and other plants. They became close friends.

Carver devoted most of his adult life to research and teaching at Tuskegee. He died January 5, 1943, at age 78. He was buried on the school grounds near the grave of Booker T. Washington. His work changed science and agriculture forever. Carver's creative approach to research and teaching inspired many to follow in his footsteps.

◀ Carver and Henry Ford

Busy Inventor

Carver discovered a way to make synthetic rubber from sweet potatoes. He suggested that material for paving highways could be made from cotton. Carver also found more than 75 uses for the pecan.

Geobiologist: Hope Jahren

University of Hawaii

Time Traveler

To understand ancient plants, Hope Jahren collects plant fossils and takes them to her lab. There she studies the fossils using microscopes and other tools. Her research tells us about the air, soil, and water that the plants lived in. All these clues help Jahren understand what the climate was like long ago. With this information, we may be able to tell how the climate will change in the future.

Jahren spent three summers in the Arctic studying a 45-million-year-old fossil forest.

What was our planet like 45 million years ago? "This was a very different Earth," Jahren says. Back then the Arctic was home to a forest of huge redwood trees. The polar region wasn't icy, as it is today, but it was still dark four months a year. If you put your houseplants in a dark closet for that long, they will die. So how did a forest survive? Stay tuned—Dr. Jahren is on the case.

Fossils are one way of learning about life long ago.

Experts Tell Us

How surprising is it to find that huge trees survived those long, dark winters near the North Pole? "This is like finding a human being that could live underwater."

As a Team

"Working together is a huge part of science," Jahren says. "It's like you're part of a family that's trying to find things out."

30

Name:	George Washington Carver
Date of birth:	c. 1865
Nationality:	American
Birthplace:	Diamond Grove, Missouri
Parents:	Mary; father's name unknown
Siblings:	Jim (1859–1883)
Date of death:	January 5, 1943
Place of burial:	Tuskegee, Alabama
Fields of study:	Agricultural sciences, botany
Contributions to science:	Developed new uses for peanuts, sweet potatoes, pecans, and soybeans; studied crop rotation and improved farming practices
Publications:	More than 44 pamphlets on good farming practices and practical uses for common crops

c. 1865	George Washington Carver is born a slave near Diamond Grove, Missouri
1865	Kidnapped, along with mother, by slave raiders
1880	Moves to Minneapolis, Kansas
1890	Enters Simpson College in Iowa as an art student
1891	Transfers to Iowa State College to study agricultural science
1893	Wins honorable mention at Chicago World's Fair for his painting of cactus and yucca plants
1894	Earns a degree in agricultural science and begins working at Iowa State College
1896	Earns a master's degree from Iowa State College; begins working at Tuskegee Institute
1906	Travels through Alabama with the Jesup agricultural wagon to teach poor farmers better methods of agriculture
1916	Named a Fellow of the Royal Society for the Arts for his contributions to agricultural research
1923	Awarded the Springarn Medal from the NAACP for distinguished service to science
1925	Receives patents for cosmetics and for stain and paint
1927	Receives another patent for stain and paint
1935	Begins studies of fungi for the U.S. Department of Agriculture

1937	Meets automaker Henry Ford at a conference in Michigan; the two become close friends
1938	The motion picture *The Life of George Washington Carver* is released by Hollywood
1939	Awarded the Roosevelt Medal for his contributions to science; receives an honorary membership to the American Inventors Society
1941	With financial aid from Henry Ford, the George Washington Carver Museum is dedicated at Tuskegee Institute
1943	Dies January 5 at the age of 78; buried in Tuskegee, Alabama
1946	President Harry S. Truman declares January 5 George Washington Carver Day
1947	Featured on a 3-cent commemorative stamp from the U.S. Post Office
1952	Chosen by *Popular Mechanics* as one of 50 outstanding Americans
1990	Inducted into the National Inventors Hall of Fame in Alexandria, Virginia
1998	Featured with a peanut plant and microscope on a 32-cent commemorative stamp
1999	The George Washington Carver Center is dedicated at the U.S. Department of Agriculture in Beltsville, Maryland

Important People in Botany

Aristotle (384 B.C.–322 B.C.)
Greek philosopher who collected a large amount of information about plants and animals and has been called the world's first important biologist

Charles Barnes (1858–1910)
American plant biologist who first suggested using the term photosynthesis to describe the way a plant converts sunlight and nutrients into food

Giovanni Battista Amici (1786–1863)
Italian scientist who showed that flowering plants reproduce sexually, which makes possible the creation of hybrid plants

Hieronymus Bock (1498–1554)
German scientist known as one of the three founding fathers of botany; noted for beginning the modern practice of sorting plants by their relation or resemblance to one another

Andrei Bolotov (1738–1833)
Russian agriculturist who wrote manuals on crop rotation and cross-pollination

Otto Brunfels (c. 1488–1534)
German scientist known as one of the founding fathers of botany; he studied and described many types of plants

Luther Burbank (1849–1926)
American plant breeder who developed more than 800 new types of plants, including fruits, flowers, grains, grasses, and vegetables

Jane Colden (1724–1766)
The first female American botanist; she collected and categorized more than 300 types of plants from the lower Hudson River Valley in New York

Abu al-Dinawari (c. 815–896)
Arabic scientist who first described the phases of plant growth from birth to death; also experimented with various types of soil

Henri Dutrochet (1776–1847)
French scientist who recognized that chlorophyll was necessary for photosynthesis

Leonhart Fuchs (1501–1566)
German scientist considered to be one of the three founding fathers of botany; the flowering plant fuchsia is named for him

Nehemiah Grew (1641–1712)
English scientist who studied the anatomy of vegetables; published the *Anatomy of Plants* in 1682

Stephen Hales (1677–1761)
English botanist who studied the importance of air and water to plant and animal life and showed that plants absorb air

Alexander von Humboldt (1769–1859)
German scientist who pioneered the idea of writing about plants based on their location, also known as botanical geography; known as the father of ecology

Jan Ingenhousz (1730–1799)
Dutch-born English scientist who discovered photosynthesis

Justus von Liebig (1803–1873)
German chemist who was a pioneer in organic chemistry; known as the father of the fertilizer industry for his discovery that nitrogen is an important plant nutrient; developed the modern laboratory method of teaching science

Carl Linnaeus (1707–1778)
Swedish botanist who divided the plant kingdom into 25 classes and created the first logical and systematic way to classify all living things; after some changes, it became the standard system

Alice Lounsberry (1872–1949)
American botanist and author of several books on plants, including *A Guide to the Wild Flowers*

Pliny the Elder (23–79)
Roman naturalist whose encyclopedia *Historia Naturalis* (Natural History) included 16 volumes on plants

Joseph Priestley (1733–1804)
English scientist who showed that plants in sunlight give off oxygen and "restore" air that lacks oxygen because of burning or the breathing of animals

Ellis Rowan (1847–1922)
Australian botanical artist known for her detailed and accurate drawings of various plants; she created illustrations for three books written by American botanist Alice Lounsberry

Julius von Sachs (1832–1897)
German botanist who founded the scientific study of plant physiology (how plant processes work)

Dunkinfield Henry Scott (1854–1934)
English scientist who pioneered the study of fossil plants

Jean Senebier (1742–1809)
Swiss botanist who discovered that green plants, using light, take in carbon dioxide and give off oxygen

Theophrastus (c. 372 B.C.–c. 287 B.C.)
Greek philosopher who named and classified many plants based on information gathered by his teacher, Aristotle

Eli Whitney (1765–1825)
American inventor who created the cotton gin, a machine that revolutionized the processing of cotton and led to cotton's becoming the foundation of the South's economy

Karl Wilhelm von Nägeli (1817–1891)
Swiss botanist who as a young man wrote a paper accurately describing the division of cells; he and Hugo von Mohl, a German botanist, first noted the differences between plant cell walls and their interiors

Glossary

abolitionist—person who supported the banning of slavery

agricultural biochemist—scientist who studies the chemistry of plants

anatomy—study of the physical structure of plants or animals

botany—study of plants and plant life

briquette—molded block of coal or charcoal used for fuel

chemurgist—scientist who tries to find industrial or commercial uses for farm products

crop rotation—growing a different crop in the same field each year to avoid damaging the soil

crossbreeding—creating new types of plants or animals by mixing two types

ecology—study of relationships among plants, animals, and their environment

eroded—worn away by wind, water, or ice

geobiologist—scientist who specializes in geology (the study of Earth's formation and changes) and biology (the study of living things)

Jesup agricultural wagon—horse-drawn vehicle used by Carver to teach on farms

linoleum—sturdy, washable floor covering

nutrients—substances that provide nourishment for living things

patent—exclusive right, granted by a government, to an inventor to make or sell an invention

plantation—large farm in the South, usually worked by slaves

pleats—flat, narrow folds in cloth

pollen—powdery substance made by flowering plants for fertilizing other plants

prejudice—irrational hatred, fear, or mistrust of a person or group, often because of their race or religion

protein—chemical made by animal and plant cells to carry out various functions

segregated—separated by race

synthetic—artificial or manufactured; not created by nature

Additional Resources

Bolden, Tonya. *George Washington Carver*. New York: Abrams Books for Young Readers, 2008.

Burgan, Michael. *George Washington Carver: Scientist, Inventor, and Teacher*. Minneapolis: Compass Point Books, 2007.

Casper, Julie Kerr. *Plants: Life From the Earth*. New York: Chelsea House, 2007.

Harness, Cheryl. *The Groundbreaking, Chance-Taking Life of George Washington Carver and Science & Invention in America*. Washington, D.C.: National Geographic Society, 2008.

Krensky, Stephen. *A Man for All Seasons: The Life of George Washington Carver*. New York: HarperCollins Publishers, 2008.

Internet Sites

FactHound offers a safe, fun way to find Internet sites related to this book. All of the sites on FactHound have been researched by our staff.

Here's all you do:
   Visit *www.facthound.com*
FactHound will fetch the best sites for you!

Index

Stephanie Macceca

Stephanie Macceca has been an educator at the high school and university levels for more than 15 years, with a passion for environmental science, ecology, and marine biology. She enjoys reading science fiction, has a home that runs on solar energy, and is the proud owner of an alternative-fuel vehicle. Her two children, Jack and Madeleine, plan to be scientists in the future.

Image Credits